HIGH TEA

Published in 2010 by ACP Books, Sydney

ACP Books are published by ACP Magazines a division of PBL Media Pty Limited

acp books

ACP BOOKS

General manager Christine Whiston
Editor-in-chief Susan Tomnay
Creative director Hieu Chi Nguyen
Art director & designer Hannah Blackmore
Senior editor Stephanie Kistner
Food director Pamela Clark
Sales & rights director Brian Cearnes
Marketing manager Bridget Cody
Senior business analyst Rebecca Varela
Operations manager David Scotto
Production manager Victoria Jefferys

Published by ACP Books, a division of ACP Magazines Ltd, 54 Park St, Sydney; GPO Box 4088, Sydney, NSW 2001. phone (02) 9282 8618; fax (02) 9267 9438.

acpbooks@acpmagazines.com.au; www.acpbooks.com.au

The publishers would like to thank the following for props used in photography:
That Vintage Shop www.thatvintageshop.com.au;
Waterford Wedgwood www.waterfordwedgwood.com.au;
Le Forge www.leforge.com.au;
Porters Paints and Wallpapers www.porterspaints.com.au;
Publisher textiles www.publishertextiles.com.au;
Imagine This www.imagine-this.com.au;
Trovata Pty Ltd www.trovata.com.au;
Pigott's store www.pigotts.com.au;
Reclaim www.reclaim.net.au;
Peter's of Kensington www.pertersofkensington.com.au

Printed by C&C Offset Printing, China.

Australia Distributed by Network Services, phone +61 2 9282 8777; fax +61 2 9264 3278; networkweb@networkservicescompany.com.au
United Kingdom Distributed by Australian Consolidated Press (UK), phone (01604) 642 200; fax (01604) 642 300; books@acpuk.com
New Zealand Distributed by Southern Publishers Group, phone (9) 360 0692; fax (9) 360 0695; hub@spg.co.nz
South Africa Distributed by PSD Promotions, phone (27 11) 392 6065/6/7; fax (27 11) 392 6079/80; orders@psdprom.co.za
Canada Distributed by Publishers Group Canada phone (800) 663 5714; fax (800) 565 3770; service@raincoast.com

High tea / food director Pamela Clark.
ISBN: 978-1-86396-988-8 (hbk.)
Notes: Includes index.
Subjects: Afternoon teas. Cake. Baking.
Other Authors/Contributors: Clark, Pamela.
Also Titled: Australian women's weekly.
Dewey Number: 641.536

Food editor Alexandra Elliott
Recipe development Nicole Jennings
Photographer Louise Lister
Stylist Vicki Liley
Food preparation Nicole Jennings, Rebecca Squadrito
Front cover (clockwise from back) Orange almond victoria sponge, page 112; Neenish & pineapple tarts, page 39; Custard fruit flans, page 40.
Front flap Fig & walnut friands, page 94.
Back cover (from left to right) Fruit mince pies with spiced hazelnut pastry, page 47; Pistachio, white chocolate and honey french macaroons, page 62; Orange & almond palmiers, page 35.

Scanpan cookware is used in the AWW Test Kitchen.

To order books
phone 136 116 (within Australia) or
order online at www.acpbooks.com.au
Send recipe enquiries to: recipeenquiries@acpmagazines.com.au

THE AUSTRALIAN Women's Weekly

HIGH TEA

acp books

CONTENTS

There are few hours in life more agreeable than the hour dedicated to the ceremony known as afternoon tea.

– HENRY JAMES THE PORTRAIT OF A LADY

SANDWICHES

MARINATED CUCUMBER

- 2 lebanese cucumbers (260g/8 ounces), sliced thinly lengthways
- 1 tablespoon white wine vinegar
- 1 tablespoon finely chopped fresh dill
- ½ teaspoon sea salt flakes
- ½ teaspoon caster (superfine) sugar
- ¼ teaspoon cracked black pepper
- 30g (1 ounce) butter, softened
- 8 slices wholemeal bread (360g)
- ½ cup (120g) crème fraîche

1 Combine cucumber, vinegar, dill, salt, sugar and pepper in medium bowl. Cover; refrigerate 2 hours.
2 Drain cucumber; discard excess liquid.
3 Spread butter over bread slices. Spread crème fraîche over half the buttered bread slices; top slices with cucumber then remaining bread. Discard crusts; cut each sandwich into four finger sandwiches.

prep time 20 minutes (+ refrigeration)
makes 16
tip The cucumber can be sliced with a vegetable peeler for even, thin slices.

CREAMY EGG & WATERCRESS

- 3 hard-boiled eggs, mashed
- ¼ cup (75g) whole-egg mayonnaise
- 1 teaspoon dijon mustard
- 1 tablespoon finely chopped fresh chives
- 1 tablespoon finely chopped fresh flat-leaf parsley
- 30g (1 ounce) butter, softened
- 8 slices white bread (360g)
- 1 cup (20g) loosely packed watercress sprigs

1 Combine eggs, mayonnaise, mustard and herbs in medium bowl. Season to taste.
2 Spread butter over bread slices; top half the slices with egg mixture and watercress then remaining bread. Discard crusts; cut each sandwich into four finger sandwiches.

prep time 20 minutes
makes 16

SALMON & HERBED CREAM CHEESE

60g (2 ounces) cream cheese, softened
2 teaspoons finely chopped fresh dill
2 teaspoons finely chopped fresh chives
2 teaspoons lemon juice
1 teaspoon drained baby capers, rinsed, chopped finely
4 slices white bread (180g), crusts removed
125g (4 ounces) smoked salmon
4 large rocket (arugula) leaves, trimmed

1 Combine cream cheese, dill, chives, juice and capers in small bowl. Season to taste.
2 Using rolling pin, roll over one slice of bread to flatten slightly. Spread with a quarter of the cream cheese mixture; top with a quarter of the smoked salmon and one rocket leaf, roll tightly to enclose filling. Repeat with remaining bread, cream cheese mixture, smoked salmon and rocket. Trim ends then cut each roll into four slices.

prep time 20 minutes
makes 16

CHICKEN & ALMOND

1 cup (250ml) chicken stock
1 cup (250ml) water
6 black peppercorns
1 bay leaf
250g (8 ounces) chicken breast
1 stalk celery (150g), trimmed, chopped finely
2 tablespoons flaked almonds, roasted
¼ cup (60g) crème fraîche
2 tablespoons whole-egg mayonnaise
1 teaspoon lemon juice
2 teaspoons finely chopped fresh tarragon
30g (1 ounce) butter, softened
8 slices light rye bread (360g)

1 Combine stock, the water, peppercorns, bay leaf and chicken in small saucepan; bring to the boil. Reduce heat; simmer, uncovered, about 15 minutes or until chicken is cooked through, turning chicken halfway through cooking time. Remove chicken from poaching liquid. When cool enough to handle, chop chicken finely.
2 Combine chicken in medium bowl with celery, nuts, crème fraîche, mayonnaise, juice and tarragon. Season to taste.
3 Spread butter over bread slices; top half the slices with chicken mixture then remaining bread. Discard crusts; cut each sandwich into three finger sandwiches, then cut each in half crossways into squares.

prep + cook time 35 minutes (+ cooling)
makes 24

PRAWN WITH LIME & PEPPER AÏOLI

16 medium cooked king prawns (shrimp) (720g)
30g (1 ounce) butter, softened
8 slices white bread (360g)
1 cup (60g) shredded baby cos (Romaine) lettuce
lime & pepper aïoli
½ cup (150g) whole-egg mayonnaise
1 small clove garlic, crushed
½ teaspoon finely grated lime rind (peel)
2 teaspoons lime juice
¼ teaspoon cracked black pepper

1 Make lime & pepper aïoli.
2 Shell and devein prawns; halve lengthways. Stir prawns into aïoli. Season to taste.
3 Spread butter over bread slices; top half the slices with prawn mixture and shredded lettuce then remaining bread. Discard crusts; cut each sandwich into four triangles.
lime & pepper aïoli Combine ingredients in medium bowl. Season to taste.

prep time 25 minutes
makes 16

RADISH WITH GREEN ONION BUTTER

90g (3 ounces) butter, softened
2 drained anchovy fillets, crushed
1 green onion (scallion), chopped finely
1 teaspoon dijon mustard
12 slices white bread (540g)
10 trimmed radishes (150g), sliced thinly

1 Combine butter, anchovy, onion and mustard in small bowl. Season to taste.
2 Spread butter mixture over one side of eight slices of bread and over both sides of four slices of bread.
3 Top four slices of the bread buttered on one side with half the radish; top with the bread buttered on both sides. Top with remaining radish and bread (see page 122). Discard crusts; cut each sandwich into four triangles.

prep time 30 minutes
makes 16

If you are cold, tea will warm you.
If you are too heated, it will cool you.
If you are depressed, it will cheer you.
If you are excited, it will calm you.

– WILLIAM GLADSTONE FOUR TIMES PRIME MINISTER OF THE UNITED KINGDOM

SCONES

SCONES WITH JAM & CREAM

2½ cups (375g) self-raising flour
1 tablespoon caster (superfine) sugar
30g (1 ounce) butter, chopped
1¼ cups (310ml) buttermilk
¾ cup (240g) black cherry jam
1 cup (250ml) double cream

1 Preheat oven to 200°C/400°F. Grease 22cm (9-inch) square cake pan.
2 Sift flour and sugar into large bowl; rub in butter.
3 Add buttermilk. Use a knife to cut the buttermilk through the flour mixture to make a soft, sticky dough. Turn dough onto floured surface, knead gently until smooth.
4 Press dough out to 2cm (¾ inch) thickness, cut out 4cm (1½ inch) rounds. Place scones, just touching, in pan. Gently knead scraps of dough together; repeat process. Brush scones with a little extra buttermilk.
5 Bake scones about 15 minutes. Serve warm scones with jam and cream.

prep + cook time 35 minutes
makes 25
tips Scones are best made on the day of serving. They can be frozen for up to 3 months. Thaw in oven, wrapped in foil.
You could substitute the double cream for clotted cream or whipped thickened cream.

VANILLA BEAN SCONES

2½ cups (375g) self-raising flour
1 tablespoon caster (superfine) sugar
30g (1 ounce) butter, chopped
¾ cup (180ml) milk
½ cup (125ml) water
1 vanilla bean
1¼ cups (300ml) thickened (heavy) cream
2 tablespoons icing (confectioners') sugar
¾ cup (240g) strawberry jam
250g (8 ounces) strawberries, sliced thinly

1 Preheat oven to 200°C/400°F. Grease 22cm (9-inch) square cake pan.
2 Sift flour and caster sugar into large bowl; rub in butter.
3 Combine milk and the water in a medium jug. Split vanilla bean open and scrape seeds into milk mixture; discard bean. Add milk mixture to flour mixture; use a knife to cut the milk mixture through the flour mixture to make a soft, sticky dough. Turn dough onto floured surface, knead gently until smooth.
4 Press dough out to 20cm (8-inch) square, cut into 16 squares (see page 122) using floured knife. Place squares, just touching, in pan. Brush scones with a little extra milk.
5 Bake scones about 20 minutes.
6 Meanwhile, beat cream and half the sifted icing sugar in small bowl with electric mixer until soft peaks form.
7 Sandwich warm scones with jam, strawberries and cream; serve dusted with remaining sifted icing sugar.

prep + cook time 40 minutes
makes 16
tip Scones are best made on the day of serving. They can be frozen for up to 3 months. Thaw in oven, wrapped in foil.

DATE SCONES WITH WHIPPED CARAMEL BUTTER

30g (1 ounce) butter, softened
¼ cup (55g) firmly packed brown sugar
1 egg yolk
2½ cups (375g) self-raising flour
⅓ cup (50g) finely chopped seeded dried dates
1¼ cups (310ml) buttermilk

whipped caramel butter

150g (5 ounces) unsalted butter, softened
¼ cup (55g) brown sugar
2 teaspoons vanilla extract

1 Preheat oven to 200°C/400°F. Grease 22cm (9-inch) square cake pan.
2 Beat butter, sugar and egg yolk in small bowl with electric mixer until light and fluffy. Transfer mixture to large bowl; add sifted flour, dates and buttermilk. Use a knife to cut the buttermilk through the flour mixture to make a soft, sticky dough. Turn dough onto floured surface, knead gently until smooth.
3 Press dough out to 20cm (8-inch) square, cut into 9 squares, using a floured knife, then cut each square in half diagonally (see page 122). Place scones side by side, just touching, in pan. Brush scones with a little extra buttermilk.
4 Bake scones about 20 minutes.
5 Meanwhile, make whipped caramel butter.
6 Serve warm scones with whipped caramel butter.

whipped caramel butter Beat ingredients in small bowl with electric mixer until light and fluffy.

prep + cook time 40 minutes
makes 18
tip Scones are best made on the day of serving. They can be frozen for up to 3 months. Thaw in oven, wrapped in foil.

GINGERBREAD SCONES WITH LEMON GLACE ICING

30g (1 ounce) butter, softened
¼ cup (55g) firmly packed brown sugar
1 egg yolk
2½ cups (375g) self-raising flour
3 teaspoons ground ginger
1½ teaspoons ground cinnamon
¼ teaspoon ground clove
1 cup (250ml) buttermilk
2 tablespoons treacle or golden syrup

lemon glacé icing

1 cup (160g) icing (confectioners') sugar
15g (½ ounce) butter, melted
1 tablespoon lemon juice

1 Preheat oven to 200°C/400°F. Grease 22cm (9-inch) square cake pan.

2 Beat butter, sugar and egg yolk in small bowl with electric mixer until light and fluffy. Transfer mixture to large bowl; add sifted dry ingredients and combined buttermilk and treacle. Use a knife to cut the buttermilk mixture through flour mixture to make a soft, sticky dough. Turn dough onto floured surface, knead gently until smooth.

3 Press dough out to 2cm (¾ inch) thickness, cut into 5cm (2 inch) rounds. Place rounds, just touching, in pan. Gently knead scraps of dough together; repeat process. Brush scones with a little extra buttermilk.

4 Bake scones about 20 minutes. Cool 10 minutes.

5 Meanwhile, make lemon glacé icing.

6 Serve warm scones drizzled with icing and decorated with shredded lemon rind, if you like.

lemon glacé icing Sift icing sugar into small heatproof bowl; stir in butter and enough juice to make a thick paste. Place bowl over small saucepan of simmering water; stir until mixture is smooth.

prep + cook time 40 minutes
makes 16
tips Scones are best made on the day of serving. They can be frozen for up to 3 months. Thaw in oven, wrapped in foil.
Use a zester to shred lemon rind.

PUMPKIN PARMESAN SCONES

30g (1 ounce) butter, softened
¼ cup (40g) icing (confectioners') sugar
1 egg
¾ cup cold cooked mashed pumpkin
2½ cups (375g) self-raising flour
½ teaspoon ground nutmeg
⅓ cup (80ml) milk, approximately
2 tablespoons finely grated parmesan cheese
pinch cracked black pepper
pinch sea salt flakes

1 Preheat oven to 200°C/400°F. Grease 22cm (9-inch) square cake pan.
2 Beat butter, sugar and egg in small bowl with electric mixer until light and fluffy. Transfer mixture to large bowl; stir in pumpkin. Add sifted dry ingredients and milk. Use a knife to cut the milk through the flour mixture to make a soft, sticky dough. Turn dough onto floured surface, knead gently until smooth.
3 Press dough out to 2cm (¾ inch) thickness, cut out 5cm (2 inch) rounds. Place rounds, just touching, in pan. Gently knead scraps of dough together; repeat process.
4 Brush scones with a little extra milk; sprinkle with combined cheese, pepper and salt.
5 Bake scones about 20 minutes.
6 Serve scones warm with butter.

prep + cook time 35 minutes
makes 16
tips The amount of milk you need to add to this scone dough depends on the water content of the pumpkin. The amount you add will vary every time you make these scones.
Scones are best made on the day of serving. They can be frozen for up to 3 months. Thaw in oven, wrapped in foil.

There is no trouble so great or grave that cannot be much diminished by a nice cup of tea.

– BERNARD-PAUL HEROUX 19TH CENTURY PHILOSOPHER

PASTRIES

LIMONCELLO MERINGUE PIES

1¾ cups (260g) plain (all-purpose) flour
¼ cup (40g) icing (confectioners') sugar
185g (6 ounces) cold unsalted butter, chopped coarsely
1 egg yolk
2 teaspoons iced water, approximately
3 egg whites
¾ cup (165g) caster (superfine) sugar

limoncello curd

3 egg yolks
½ cup (110g) caster (superfine) sugar
1 teaspoon finely grated lemon rind (peel)
¼ cup (60ml) lemon juice
90g (3 ounces) cold unsalted butter, chopped
1 tablespoon limoncello liqueur

1 Make limoncello curd.

2 Process flour, icing sugar and butter until crumbly. With motor operating, add egg yolk and enough of the water to make ingredients cling together. Turn dough onto floured surface, knead gently until smooth. Wrap pastry in plastic; refrigerate 30 minutes.

3 Grease two 12-hole (1-tablespoon /20ml) mini muffin pans. Roll out half the pastry between sheets of baking paper until 5mm (¼ inch) thick. Cut out 12 x 6cm (2¼ inch) rounds; press rounds into holes of one pan. Prick base of cases well with a fork. Repeat with remaining pastry. Refrigerate 30 minutes.

4 Meanwhile, preheat oven to 200°C/400°F.

5 Bake cases about 12 minutes. Stand cases 5 minutes before transferring to wire rack to cool.

6 Beat egg whites in small bowl with electric mixer until soft peaks form. Gradually add caster sugar, beating until dissolved between additions.

7 Increase oven temperature to 220°C/425°F.

8 Divide limoncello curd into cases. Spoon meringue mixture into piping bag fitted with 1cm (½ inch) plain tube; pipe meringue over curd. Bake about 2 minutes. Cool.

limoncello curd Whisk egg yolks and sugar in medium heatproof bowl until pale and thickened slightly. Whisk in rind and juice; stir over medium saucepan of simmering water about 12 minutes or until mixture coats the back of a spoon. Remove from heat; gradually whisk in butter until combined between additions. Stir in limoncello; cover, refrigerate overnight.

prep + cook time 1 hour 15 minutes (+ refrigeration & cooling)
makes 24
tip Pastry cases and curd can be made 2 days ahead. Store the cases in an airtight container and the curd in the refrigerator.

CHOCOLATE BANOFFEE PIES

1½ cups (225g) plain (all-purpose) flour
¼ cup (40g) icing (confectioners') sugar
¼ cup (25g) cocoa powder
185g (6 ounces) cold unsalted butter, chopped coarsely
1 egg yolk
2 teaspoons iced water, approximately
1 small banana (130g), sliced thinly
⅓ cup (80ml) double cream
1 teaspoon cocoa powder, extra

chocolate caramel filling

60g (2 ounces) unsalted butter, chopped coarsely
¼ cup (55g) firmly packed brown sugar
1 cup (300g) sweetened condensed milk
30g (1 ounce) dark eating (semi-sweet) chocolate, chopped coarsely
2 teaspoons golden syrup or treacle

1 Process sifted flour, sugar and cocoa with butter until crumbly. With motor operating, add egg yolk and enough of the water to make ingredients cling together. Turn dough onto floured surface, knead gently until smooth. Wrap pastry in plastic; refrigerate 30 minutes.
2 Grease two 12-hole (1-tablespoon /20ml) mini muffin pans. Roll out half the pastry between sheets of baking paper until 5mm (¼ inch) thick. Cut out 12 x 6cm (2¼ inch) rounds; press rounds into holes of one pan. Prick base of cases well with a fork. Repeat with remaining pastry. Refrigerate 30 minutes.
3 Preheat oven to 200°C/400°F.
4 Bake cases about 12 minutes. Stand cases 5 minutes before transferring to wire rack to cool.
5 Meanwhile, make chocolate caramel filling.
6 Divide hot filling into cases; cool. Refrigerate 1 hour.
7 Top filling with banana and cream; dust with a little extra sifted cocoa.

chocolate caramel filling Stir butter and sugar in small saucepan over low heat until sugar dissolves. Add condensed milk; cook, stirring, about 5 minutes until mixture boils and thickens. Remove from heat, stir in chocolate and syrup until smooth.

prep + cook time 1 hour 10 minutes (+ refrigeration)
makes 24
tip Pastry cases can be made 2 days ahead, store in airtight container.

CHOCOLATE ECLAIRS

15g (½ ounce) butter
¼ cup (60ml) water
¼ cup (35g) plain (all-purpose) flour
1 egg

custard cream

1 vanilla bean
1 cup (250ml) milk
3 egg yolks
⅓ cup (75g) caster (superfine) sugar
2 tablespoons pure cornflour (cornstarch)
⅓ cup (80ml) thickened (heavy) cream, whipped

chocolate glaze

30g (1 ounce) dark eating (semi-sweet) chocolate, chopped coarsely
30g (1 ounce) milk eating chocolate, chopped coarsely
15g (½ ounce) butter

1 Make custard cream.
2 Preheat oven to 200°C/400°F. Grease two oven trays.
3 Combine butter and the water in small saucepan; bring to the boil. Add flour, beat with wooden spoon over heat until mixture comes away from base and side of pan and forms a smooth ball.
4 Transfer mixture to small bowl; beat in egg with electric mixer until mixture becomes glossy. Spoon pastry mixture into piping bag fitted with 1cm (½ inch) plain tube. Pipe 5cm (2 inch) lengths about 5cm (2 inch) apart on trays; bake for 7 minutes. Reduce oven temperature to 160°C/325°F; bake further 10 minutes. Using serrated knife, cut éclairs in half, remove any soft centres; return to trays, bake further 5 minutes or until dry to touch. Cool on trays.
5 Make chocolate glaze.
6 Spoon custard cream into piping bag fitted with 5mm (¼ inch) fluted tube. Pipe custard cream into 16 pastry bases, top with pastry tops. Spread with chocolate glaze.

custard cream Split vanilla bean, scrape seeds into milk in small saucepan (discard bean); bring to the boil. Meanwhile, beat egg yolks, sugar and cornflour in small bowl with electric mixer until thick. With motor operating, gradually beat in hot milk mixture. Return custard to pan; stir over heat until mixture boils and thickens. Cover surface of custard with plastic wrap, refrigerate 1 hour. Fold cream into custard in two batches.

chocolate glaze Stir ingredients in small heatproof bowl over small saucepan of simmering water until smooth. Use while warm.

prep + cook time 1 hour (+ refrigeration & cooling)
makes 16
tips Eclairs and custard cream can be made and stored separately, 2 days ahead; fold cream into custard just before using. Assemble and serve éclairs as close to serving time as possible – about an hour is good.

ORANGE & ALMOND PALMIERS

1 cup (150g) vienna almonds
15g (½ ounce) butter
2 tablespoons orange-flavoured liqueur
2 teaspoons finely grated orange rind (peel)
2 tablespoons demerara (light brown) sugar
2 sheets butter puff pastry
1 egg, beaten lightly

orange glacé icing

1 cup (160g) icing (confectioners') sugar
15g (½ ounce) butter
½ teaspoon finely grated orange rind (peel)
2 teaspoons orange juice
2 teaspoons hot water, approximately

1 Blend or process nuts, butter, liqueur and rind to a coarse paste.
2 Sprinkle board with half the sugar; place one sheet of pastry on the sugar. Roll pastry gently into sugar (see page 123). Spread half the nut mixture over pastry; fold two opposite sides of pastry inwards to meet in the middle (see page 123). Flatten folded pastry slightly; brush with a little egg. Fold each side in half to meet in the middle; flatten slightly. Fold the two sides in half again so they touch in the middle (see page 123). Repeat process with remaining sugar, pastry, nut mixture and egg. Cover pastry rolls; refrigerate 30 minutes.
3 Preheat oven to 180°C/350°F. Grease two oven trays.
4 Cut pastry rolls into 1cm (½ inch) slices; place slices about 2.5cm (1 inch) apart on trays.
5 Bake palmiers about 12 minutes. Transfer to wire racks to cool.
6 Meanwhile, make orange glacé icing.
7 Spread one side of palmiers with icing; set at room temperature.

orange glacé icing Sift icing sugar into small heatproof bowl; stir in butter, rind, juice and enough of the water to make a thick paste. Place bowl over small saucepan of simmering water; stir until icing is spreadable.

prep + cook time 45 minutes (+ refrigeration)
makes 32

MASCARPONE & PAPAYA TARTS

1¾ cups (260g) plain (all-purpose) flour
¼ cup (40g) icing (confectioners') sugar
185g (6 ounces) cold butter, chopped coarsely
2 tablespoons finely chopped glacé ginger
1 egg yolk
2 teaspoons iced water, approximately
½ small papaya (325g), seeded

mascarpone filling

250g (8 ounces) mascarpone cheese
⅓ cup (80ml) thickened (heavy) cream
2 tablespoons honey
¼ cup (70g) mashed papaya
1 tablespoon lime juice

1 Process flour, sugar, butter and ginger until crumbly. With motor operating, add egg yolk and enough of the water to make ingredients come together. Turn dough onto floured surface, knead gently until smooth. Wrap pastry in plastic; refrigerate 30 minutes.
2 Grease two 12-hole (2-tablespoons/40ml) deep flat-based patty pans. Roll out half the pastry between sheets of baking paper until 3mm (⅛ inch) thick. Cut out 12 x 7.5cm (3 inch) rounds; press pastry rounds into holes of one pan. Prick base of cases well with a fork. Repeat with remaining pastry. Refrigerate 30 minutes.
3 Preheat oven to 200°C/400°F.
4 Bake cases about 12 minutes. Stand cases 5 minutes before transferring to wire rack to cool.
5 Meanwhile, make mascarpone filling.
6 Using vegetable peeler, slice papaya into small thin strips. Divide mascarpone filling into cases; top with papaya.

mascarpone filling Beat mascarpone, cream and honey in small bowl with electric mixer until smooth. Fold in papaya and juice.

prep + cook time 55 minutes (+ refrigeration & cooling)
makes 24
tip You will need 1 small papaya (650g) for this recipe.

NEENISH & PINEAPPLE TARTS

1¾ cups (260g) plain (all-purpose) flour
¼ cup (40g) icing (confectioners') sugar
185g (6 ounces) cold butter, chopped coarsely
1 egg yolk
2 teaspoons iced water, approximately
2 tablespoons strawberry jam
2 tablespoons finely chopped glacé pineapple

mock cream

¾ cup (165g) caster (superfine) sugar
⅓ cup (80ml) water
1½ tablespoons milk
½ teaspoon gelatine
185g (6 ounces) unsalted butter, softened
1 teaspoon vanilla extract

glacé icing

1½ cups (240g) icing (confectioners') sugar
15g (½ ounce) unsalted butter, melted
2 tablespoons hot milk, approximately
yellow and pink food colouring
½ teaspoon cocoa powder

1 Process flour, sugar and butter until crumbly. With motor operating, add egg yolk and enough of the water to make ingredients come together. Turn dough onto floured surface, knead gently until smooth. Wrap pastry in plastic; refrigerate 30 minutes.

2 Grease two 12-hole (2-tablespoons /40ml) deep flat-based patty pans. Roll out half the pastry between sheets of baking paper until 3mm (⅛ inch) thick. Cut out 12 x 7.5cm (3 inch) rounds; press rounds into holes of one pan. Prick bases of cases well with a fork. Repeat with remaining pastry. Refrigerate 30 minutes.

3 Preheat oven to 200°C/400°F.

4 Bake cases about 12 minutes. Stand cases 5 minutes before transferring to wire rack to cool.

5 Meanwhile, make mock cream and glacé icing.

6 Divide jam between half the cases and pineapple between remaining cases. Fill cases with mock cream, level tops with spatula. Spread yellow icing over pineapple tarts. Spread pink icing over half of each jam tart; cover remaining half with chocolate icing.

mock cream Stir sugar, ¼ cup of the water and milk in small saucepan over low heat, without boiling, until sugar dissolves. Sprinkle gelatine over remaining water in small jug; stir into milk mixture until gelatine dissolves. Cool to room temperature. Beat butter and extract in small bowl with electric mixer until as white as possible. While motor is operating, gradually beat in cold milk mixture; beat until light and fluffy.

glacé icing Sift icing sugar into medium bowl; stir in butter and enough of the milk to make a thick paste. Place ⅓ cup of the icing in small heatproof bowl; tint with yellow colouring. Divide remaining icing between two small heatproof bowls; tint icing in one bowl with pink colouring and the other with sifted cocoa. Stir each bowl over small saucepan of simmering water until icing is spreadable.

prep + cook time 1 hour 10 minutes (+ refrigeration & cooling)
makes 24

CUSTARD FRUIT FLANS

- 1¾ cups (260g) plain (all-purpose) flour
- ¼ cup (40g) icing (confectioners') sugar
- 185g (6 ounces) cold butter, chopped coarsely
- 1 egg yolk
- 2 teaspoons iced water, approximately
- 1 medium kiwifruit (85g)
- 60g (2 ounces) fresh raspberries, halved
- 60g (2 ounces) fresh blueberries

custard cream

- 1 cup (250ml) milk
- 1 teaspoon vanilla extract
- 3 egg yolks
- ⅓ cup (75g) caster (superfine) sugar
- 2 tablespoons pure cornflour (cornstarch)
- ⅓ cup (80ml) thickened (heavy) cream, whipped

1 Process flour, sugar and butter until crumbly. With motor operating, add egg yolk and enough of the water to make ingredients come together. Turn dough onto floured surface, knead gently until smooth. Wrap pastry in plastic; refrigerate 30 minutes.

2 Grease two 12-hole (1-tablespoon /20ml) mini muffin pans. Roll out half the pastry between sheets of baking paper until 3mm (⅛ inch) thick. Cut out 12 x 6cm (2¼ inch) rounds; press rounds into holes of one pan. Prick bases of cases well with a fork. Repeat with remaining pastry. Refrigerate 30 minutes.

3 Preheat oven to 200°C/400°F.

4 Bake cases about 12 minutes. Stand cases 5 minutes, before transferring to wire rack to cool.

5 Meanwhile, make custard cream.

6 Cut kiwifruit crossways into eight slices; cut 3cm (1 inch) rounds from slices. Divide custard cream into cases; top with fruit.

custard cream Combine milk and extract in small saucepan; bring to the boil. Meanwhile, beat egg yolks, sugar and cornflour in small bowl with electric mixer until thick. With motor operating, gradually beat in hot milk mixture. Return custard to pan; stir over heat until mixture boils and thickens. Cover surface of custard with plastic wrap, refrigerate 1 hour. Fold cream into custard in two batches.

prep + cook time 1 hour (+ refrigeration & cooling)
makes 24
tip Pastry cases and custard cream can be made and stored separately, 2 days ahead; fold cream into custard just before using. Assemble and serve flans as close to serving time as possible – about an hour is good.

PASSIONFRUIT CURD & COCONUT TARTS

1¾ cups (260g) plain (all-purpose) flour
¼ cup (40g) icing (confectioners') sugar
¼ cup (20g) desiccated coconut
185g (6 ounces) cold unsalted butter, chopped coarsely
1 egg yolk
2 teaspoons iced water, approximately
1 small coconut (700g)

passionfruit curd

⅓ cup (80ml) passionfruit pulp
½ cup (110g) caster (superfine) sugar
2 eggs, beaten lightly
125g (4 ounces) unsalted butter, chopped coarsely

1 Make passionfruit curd.

2 Process flour, sugar, desiccated coconut and butter until crumbly. With motor operating, add egg yolk and enough of the water to make ingredients come together. Turn dough onto floured surface, knead gently until smooth. Wrap pastry in plastic; refrigerate 30 minutes.

3 Grease two 12-hole (2-tablespoons /40ml) deep flat-based patty pans. Roll out half the pastry between sheets of baking paper until 5mm (¼ inch) thick. Cut out 12 x 7.5cm (3 inch) rounds; press rounds into holes of one pan. Prick bases of cases well with a fork. Repeat with remaining pastry. Refrigerate 30 minutes.

4 Preheat oven to 200°C/400°F.

5 Bake cases about 12 minutes or until browned. Stand cases 5 minutes before transferring to wire rack to cool.

6 Increase oven temperature to 220°C/425°F. Pierce one eye of the coconut using sharp knife; drain liquid from coconut. Place coconut on oven tray; bake about 10 minutes or until cracks appear. Carefully split the coconut open by hitting with a hammer; remove flesh. Using vegetable peeler, slice coconut into curls; reserve ½ cup coconut curls for this recipe and keep remaining for another use. Roast reserved coconut on oven tray about 5 minutes or until lightly browned.

7 Divide passionfruit curd into cases; top with coconut curls.

passionfruit curd Stir ingredients in medium heatproof bowl over medium saucepan of simmering water about 10 minutes or until mixture coats the back of a wooden spoon. Cover surface with plastic wrap; refrigerate overnight.

prep + cook time 1 hour 10 minutes (+ refrigeration & cooling)
makes 24

CHERRY BAKEWELL TARTS

90g (3 ounces) unsalted butter, softened
2 tablespoons caster (superfine) sugar
1 egg yolk
1 cup (150g) plain (all-purpose) flour
½ cup (60g) ground almonds
2 tablespoons strawberry jam
12 red glacé cherries, halved

almond filling

125g (4 ounces) unsalted butter, softened
½ teaspoon finely grated lemon rind (peel)
½ cup (110g) caster (superfine) sugar
2 eggs
¾ cup (90g) ground almonds
2 tablespoons plain (all-purpose) flour

lemon glaze

1 cup (160g) icing (confectioners') sugar
2 tablespoons lemon juice, approximately

1 Beat butter, sugar and egg yolk in small bowl with electric mixer until combined. Stir in sifted flour and ground almonds in two batches. Turn dough onto floured surface, knead gently until smooth, wrap in plastic; refrigerate 30 minutes.

2 Preheat oven to 200°C/400°F.

3 Make almond filling.

4 Grease two 12-hole (1½-tablespoons/30ml) shallow round-based patty pans. Roll pastry between sheets of baking paper until 3mm thick. Cut 24 x 6cm (2¼ inch) rounds from pastry; gently press rounds into holes in pans. Divide jam then filling into cases; bake about 20 minutes. Stand tarts 10 minutes; turn, top-side up, onto wire rack.

5 Meanwhile, make lemon glaze.

6 Spoon glaze over warm tarts; top with cherries. Cool.

almond filling Beat butter, rind and sugar in small bowl with electric mixer until light and fluffy. Beat in eggs, one at a time. Stir in ground almonds and flour.

lemon glaze Sift icing sugar into small bowl, stir in enough juice to make glaze pourable.

prep + cook time 1 hour (+ refrigeration & cooling)
makes 24

FRUIT MINCE PIES WITH SPICED HAZELNUT PASTRY

- 1½ cups (225g) plain (all-purpose) flour
- ¾ cup (75g) ground hazelnuts
- ½ cup (80g) icing (confectioners') sugar
- 2 teaspoons mixed spice
- 185g (6 ounces) cold butter, chopped coarsely
- 1 egg yolk
- 2 teaspoons iced water, approximately
- 1½ cups (375g) fruit mince
- 2 teaspoons finely grated orange rind (peel)
- 1 egg, beaten lightly

1 Process flour, ground hazelnuts, sugar, spice and butter until crumbly. With motor operating, add egg yolk and enough of the water to make ingredients come together. Turn dough onto floured surface, knead gently until smooth. Wrap prastry in plastic; refrigerate 30 minutes.

2 Preheat oven to 200°C/400°F. Grease 18 holes of two 12-hole (2-tablespoons/40ml) deep flat-based patty pans.

3 Roll out half the pastry between sheets of baking paper until 5mm (¼ inch) thick. Cut out 9 x 7.5cm (3 inch) fluted rounds; press rounds into holes. Repeat with remaining pastry.

4 Combine fruit mince and rind in medium bowl; divide mince mixture into cases, brush edges of pastry with egg. Roll scraps of pastry on floured surface, until 5mm (¼ inch) thick. Cut out 18 x 5cm (2 inch) fluted rounds. Cut 2cm (¾ inch) fluted rounds from centre of the rounds. Top pies with rounds.

5 Bake pies about 25 minutes. Stand pies 10 minutes; turn, top-side up, onto wire rack to cool. Dust with a little extra sifted icing sugar.

prep + cook time 1 hour (+ refrigeration & cooling)
makes 18

RHUBARB FRANGIPANE TARTS

1 vanilla bean
½ cup (110g) caster (superfine) sugar
¼ cup (60ml) water
10 stalks trimmed rhubarb (300g), cut into 4cm (1½ inch) lengths
40g (1½ inch) butter, softened
2 tablespoons caster (superfine) sugar, extra
½ teaspoon vanilla extract
1 egg yolk
½ cup (60g) ground almonds
2 teaspoons plain (all-purpose) flour
1 sheet butter puff pastry

1 Preheat oven to 160°C/325°F. Grease two oven trays.
2 Split vanilla bean, scrape seeds into a small saucepan; discard bean. Add sugar and the water to the pan. Stir syrup over heat, without boiling, until sugar dissolves. Combine rhubarb and syrup in medium baking dish; bake, uncovered, 15 minutes or until rhubarb is tender. Cool. Drain rhubarb; reserve syrup.
3 Meanwhile, beat butter, extra sugar, extract and egg yolk in small bowl with electric mixer until light and fluffy. Stir in ground almonds and flour.
4 Cut pastry into quarters; cut each quarter into three rectangles (see page 122). Place pastry rectangles about 5cm (2 inch) apart on trays; spread rounded teaspoons of almond mixture over each rectangle, leaving a 5mm (¼ inch) border. Top with rhubarb; fold pastry edges in towards centre to form raised border (see page 122).
5 Bake tarts about 25 minutes.
6 Serve tarts warm, brushed with reserved syrup.

prep + cook time 1 hour 10 minutes (+ cooling)
makes 12

LEMON CREME BRULEE TARTS

1¼ cups (300ml) (single) cream
⅓ cup (80ml) milk
4 x 5cm (2 inch) strips lemon rind (peel)
4 egg yolks
¼ cup (55g) caster (superfine) sugar

pastry

1¾ cups (260g) plain (all-purpose) flour
¼ cup (40g) icing (confectioners') sugar
2 teaspoons finely grated lemon rind (peel)
185g (6 ounces) cold butter, chopped coarsely
1 egg yolk
2 teaspoons iced water, approximately

toffee

1 cup (220g) caster (superfine) sugar
½ cup (125ml) water

1 Make pastry.

2 Grease two 12-hole (1½-tablespoons/30ml) shallow round-based patty pans. Roll half the pastry between sheets of baking paper to 3mm (⅛ inch) thickness. Cut out 12 x 6cm (2¼ inch) fluted rounds; press rounds into holes in pans. Prick bases of cases well with a fork. Repeat with remaining pastry. Refrigerate 30 minutes.

3 Preheat oven to 140°C/280°F.

4 Combine cream, milk and rind in small saucepan; bring to the boil. Beat egg yolks and sugar in small bowl with electric mixer until thick and creamy. Gradually beat hot cream mixture into egg mixture; allow bubbles to subside. Strain custard into medium jug, divide between cases; bake about 25 minutes. Cool. Refrigerate tarts 2 hours.

5 Make toffee.

6 Remove tarts from pan; place on oven tray. Sprinkle custard with toffee; using blowtorch, heat until toffee caramelises.

pastry Process flour, sugar, rind and butter until crumbly. With motor operating, add egg yolk and enough of the water to make ingredients come together. Turn dough onto floured surface, knead gently until smooth. Wrap pastry in plastic; refrigerate 30 minutes.

toffee Stir sugar and the water in medium saucepan over heat, without boiling, until sugar dissolves. Bring to the boil. Boil, uncovered, without stirring, until golden brown. Pour toffee on greased oven tray to set. Break toffee into large pieces; process until chopped finely.

prep + cook time 1 hour 10 minutes (+ refrigeration & cooling)
makes 24
tip Blowtorches are available from kitchenware and hardware stores.

PORTUGUESE CUSTARD TARTS

½ cup (110g) caster (superfine) sugar
2 tablespoons cornflour (cornstarch)
3 egg yolks
¾ cup (180ml) milk
½ cup (125ml) (single) cream
1 vanilla bean
5cm (2 inch) strip lemon rind (peel)
1 sheet butter puff pastry

1 Preheat oven to 200°C/400°F. Grease two 12-hole (1-tablespoon/20ml) mini muffin pans.

2 Combine sugar and cornflour in medium saucepan. Gradually whisk in combined egg yolks, milk and cream to make custard.

3 Split vanilla bean, scrape seeds into custard; discard bean. Add rind; stir over heat until mixture comes to the boil. Strain custard into medium jug. Cover surface of custard with plastic while making pastry cases.

4 Cut pastry sheet in half; place the two halves on top of each other. Roll pastry up tightly from long side; cut log into 24 rounds. Roll each pastry round on floured surface to 6cm (2¼ inch) diameter. Press pastry into pan holes.

5 Divide custard between cases; bake about 12 minutes. Turn tarts top-side up onto wire rack to cool. Dust with a little sifted icing sugar before serving, if you like.

prep + cook time 45 minutes
makes 24
tip Make tarts ahead (day before). Store in an airtight container. Re-crisp in 200°C/400°F oven for 5 minutes.

MOCHA PUFFS

15g (½ ounce) butter
¼ cup (60ml) water
¼ cup (35g) plain (all-purpose) flour
1 egg

mocha pastry cream

2 teaspoons instant coffee granules
2 teaspoons hot water
1 cup (250ml) milk
60g (2 ounces) dark eating (semi-sweet) chocolate, chopped finely
3 egg yolks
⅓ cup (75g) caster (superfine) sugar
1 tablespoon pure cornflour (cornstarch)

toffee

½ cup (110g) caster (superfine) sugar
¼ cup (60ml) water

1 Preheat oven to 200°C/400°F. Grease two oven trays.
2 Combine butter and the water in small saucepan; bring to the boil. Add flour, beat with wooden spoon over heat until mixture comes away from base and side of saucepan and forms a smooth ball.
3 Transfer mixture to small bowl; beat in egg with electric mixer until mixture becomes glossy. Spoon pastry mixture into piping bag fitted with 1cm (½ inch) plain tube. Pipe small rounds, about 5cm (1 inch) apart, on trays; bake for 7 minutes. Reduce oven temperature to 160°C/325°F; bake further 10 minutes. Cut small opening in side of each puff; bake further 5 minutes or until dry to touch. Cool on trays.
4 Meanwhile, make mocha pastry cream and toffee.
5 Spoon pastry cream into piping bag fitted with 5mm (¼ inch) plain tube, pipe through cuts into puffs. Place puffs on foil-covered tray; drizzle with toffee.

mocha pastry cream Dissolve coffee in the water in small jug. Combine milk, chocolate and coffee mixture in small saucepan; stir over heat, until smooth. Bring to the boil. Meanwhile, beat egg yolks, sugar and cornflour in small bowl with electric mixer until thick. With motor operating, gradually beat in hot milk mixture. Return custard to pan; stir over heat until mixture boils and thickens. Cover surface of custard with plastic wrap; refrigerate 1 hour.
toffee Combine sugar and the water in small saucepan; stir over heat, without boiling, until sugar dissolves. Bring to the boil. Boil, uncovered, without stirring, until golden brown.

prep + cook time 1 hour (+ refrigeration & cooling)
makes 24

If man has no tea in him, he is incapable of understanding truth and beauty.

– Japanese Proverb

MORSELS

MADELEINES

- 2 eggs
- 2 tablespoons caster (superfine) sugar
- 2 tablespoons icing (confectioners') sugar
- 1 teaspoon vanilla extract
- ¼ cup (35g) self-raising flour
- ¼ cup (35g) plain (all-purpose) flour
- 75g (2½ ounces) butter, melted
- 1 tablespoon hot water
- 2 tablespoons icing (confectioners') sugar, extra

1 Preheat oven to 180°C/350°F. Grease two 12-hole (1½-tablespoon /30ml) madeleine pans with a little butter.

2 Beat eggs, caster sugar, icing sugar and extract in small bowl with electric mixer until thick and creamy.

3 Meanwhile, sift flours twice. Sift flours over egg mixture; pour combined butter and the water down side of bowl then fold ingredients together.

4 Drop rounded tablespoons of mixture into pan holes.

5 Bake madeleines about 10 minutes. Tap hot pan firmly on bench to release madeleines then turn immediately onto baking-paper-covered wire racks to cool. Serve dusted with extra sifted icing sugar.

prep + cook time 25 minutes
makes 24

MACADAMIA CARAMEL SLICE

⅓ cup (50g) self-raising flour
⅓ cup (50g) plain (all-purpose) flour
¾ cup (165g) firmly packed light brown sugar
⅔ cup (50g) desiccated coconut
90g (3 ounces) butter, melted
395g (14 ounces) can sweetened condensed milk
30g (1 ounce) butter, extra
2 tablespoons golden syrup or treacle
¾ cup (105g) coarsely chopped macadamias, roasted
500g (1 pound) white eating chocolate, chopped coarsely
1 tablespoon vegetable oil
pink food colouring

1 Preheat oven to 160°C/325°F. Grease 20cm x 30cm (8 inch x 12 inch) lamington pan; line with baking paper, extending paper 5cm (2 inch) over long sides.

2 Sift flours and sugar into medium bowl, mix in coconut and butter; press mixture evenly over base of pan. Bake 15 minutes.

3 Meanwhile, stir condensed milk, extra butter and syrup in small saucepan over medium heat about 15 minutes or until caramel mixture is golden brown. Working quickly, pour caramel over base; smooth with metal spatula. Press nuts into caramel with spatula. Bake 10 minutes; cool.

4 Stir half the chocolate and oil in small saucepan over low heat until smooth. Pour chocolate mixture over caramel. Refrigerate 30 minutes.

5 Stir remaining chocolate and oil in same cleaned pan over low heat until smooth; tint with pink food colouring. Pour pink chocolate over white chocolate. Refrigerate 2 hours.

prep + cook time 50 minutes (+ cooling & refrigeration)
makes 60
tips Stand caramel slice at room temperature for at least 30 minutes before cutting into squares with sharp knife. Caramel slice can be stored, refrigerated in an airtight container, for up to 4 days.

PISTACHIO, WHITE CHOCOLATE & HONEY FRENCH MACAROONS

⅓ cup (45g) unsalted, roasted, shelled pistachios
3 egg whites
¼ cup (55g) caster (superfine) sugar
green food colouring
1¼ cups (200g) icing (confectioners') sugar
¾ cup (90g) ground almonds

honeyed white chocolate ganache

¼ cup (60ml) (single) cream
155g (5 ounces) white eating chocolate, chopped coarsely
2 teaspoons honey

1 Preheat oven to 130°C/260°F. Grease oven trays; line with baking paper.
2 Process nuts until finely ground.
3 Beat egg whites in small bowl with electric mixer until soft peaks form. Add caster sugar and few drops colouring, beat until sugar dissolves; transfer mixture to large bowl. Fold in ¼ cup of the ground pistachios, sifted icing sugar and ground almonds, in two batches.
4 Spoon mixture into piping bag fitted with 1cm (½ inch) plain tube. Pipe 4cm (1½ inch) rounds about 2.5cm (1 inch) apart onto trays. Tap trays on bench so macaroons spread slightly. Sprinkle macaroons with remaining ground pistachios; stand 30 minutes.
5 Bake macaroons about 20 minutes. Cool on trays.
6 Meanwhile, make honeyed white chocolate ganache.
7 Sandwich macaroons with ganache.

honeyed white chocolate ganache Bring cream to the boil in small saucepan. Remove from heat; pour over chocolate and honey in small bowl, stir until smooth. Stand at room temperature until spreadable.

prep + cook time 45 minutes (+ standing)
makes 16

CHOCOLATE FRENCH MACAROONS

3 egg whites
¼ cup (55g) caster (superfine) sugar
1¼ cups (200g) icing (confectioners') sugar
¾ cup (90g) ground almonds
¼ cup (25g) cocoa powder

dark chocolate ganache

¼ cup (60ml) (single) cream
155g (5 ounces) dark eating (semi-sweet) chocolate, chopped coarsely
1 tablespoon finely crushed buttered brazil nuts

1 Preheat oven to 130°C/260°F. Grease oven trays; line with baking paper.

2 Beat egg whites in small bowl with electric mixer until soft peaks form. Add caster sugar, beat until sugar dissolves; transfer mixture to large bowl. Fold in sifted icing sugar, ground almonds and sifted cocoa, in two batches.

3 Spoon mixture into piping bag fitted with 1cm (½ inch) plain tube. Pipe 4cm (1½ inch) rounds about 2.5cm (1 inch) apart onto trays. Tap trays on bench so macaroons spread slightly. Stand 30 minutes.

4 Bake macaroons about 20 minutes. Cool on trays.

5 Meanwhile, make dark chocolate ganache.

6 Sandwich macaroons with ganache.

dark chocolate ganache
Bring cream to the boil in small saucepan. Remove from heat; pour over chocolate in small bowl, stir until smooth. Stir in nuts. Stand at room temperature until spreadable.

prep + cook time 45 minutes (+ standing)
makes 16
tip Buttered brazil nuts are toffee-coated nuts; they're available from nut shops and gourmet food stores.

COCONUT FRENCH MACAROONS

3 egg whites
¼ cup (55g) caster (superfine) sugar
½ teaspoon coconut essence
1¼ cups (200g) icing (confectioners') sugar
¾ cup (90g) ground almonds
¼ cup (20g) desiccated coconut
1 tablespoon icing (confectioners') sugar, extra

white chocolate ganache

¼ cup (60ml) (single) cream
155g (5 ounces) white eating chocolate, chopped coarsely
2 teaspoons coconut-flavoured liqueur

1 Preheat oven to 130°C/260°F. Grease oven trays; line with baking paper.
2 Beat egg whites in small bowl with electric mixer until soft peaks form. Add caster sugar and essence, beat until sugar dissolves; transfer mixture to large bowl. Fold in sifted icing sugar, ground almonds and coconut, in two batches.
3 Spoon mixture into piping bag fitted with 1cm (½ inch) plain tube. Pipe 4cm (1½ inch) rounds about 2.5cm (1 inch) apart onto trays. Tap trays on bench so macaroons spread slightly. Stand 30 minutes.
4 Bake macaroons about 20 minutes. Cool on trays.
5 Meanwhile, make white chocolate ganache.
6 Sandwich macaroons with ganache. Serve dusted with extra sifted icing sugar.

white chocolate ganache
Bring cream to the boil in small saucepan. Remove from heat; pour over chocolate in small bowl, stir until smooth. Stir in liqueur. Stand at room temperature until spreadable.

prep + cook time 45 minutes (+ standing)
makes 16

STRAWBERRY FRENCH MACAROONS

3 egg whites
¼ cup (55g) caster (superfine) sugar
pink food colouring
2 large (70g) fresh or frozen strawberries
1¼ cups (200g) icing (confectioners') sugar
1 cup (120g) ground almonds
⅓ cup (110g) strawberry jam (conserve)
1 tablespoon icing (confectioners') sugar, extra

1 Preheat oven to 130°C/260°F. Grease oven trays; line with baking paper.

2 Beat egg whites in small bowl with electric mixer until soft peaks form. Add caster sugar and few drops colouring, beat until sugar dissolves; transfer mixture to large bowl.

3 Meanwhile, push fresh strawberries (or thawed frozen berries) through a fine sieve; you need 1 tablespoon of strawberry puree.

4 Fold sifted icing sugar, ground almonds and puree into egg white mixture, in two batches.

5 Spoon mixture into piping bag fitted with 1cm (½ inch) plain tube. Pipe 4cm (1½ inch) rounds about 2.5cm (1 inch) apart onto trays. Tap trays on bench so macaroons spread slightly. Stand 30 minutes.

6 Bake macaroons about 20 minutes. Cool on trays.

7 Sandwich macaroons with jam. Dust with extra sifted icing sugar.

prep + cook time 40 minutes (+ standing)
makes 16

ROSEWATER MERINGUES WITH FAIRY FLOSS

3 egg whites
¾ cup (165g) caster (superfine) sugar
2 teaspoons rosewater
1¼ cups (300ml) thickened (heavy) cream
50g rose persian fairy floss

1 Preheat oven to 100°C/210°F. Grease oven trays; line with baking paper.
2 Beat egg whites in small bowl with electric mixer until soft peaks form. Gradually add sugar, one tablespoon at a time, beating until sugar dissolves between additions. Fold in rosewater.
3 Drop heaped tablespoons of meringue mixture about 5cm (2 inch) apart onto trays; bake about 1 hour. Cool meringues in oven with door ajar.
4 Meanwhile, beat cream in small bowl with electric mixer until soft peaks form.
5 Top meringues with cream and fairy floss. Sprinkle with rose petals, if you like.

prep + cook time 1 hour 15 minutes (+ cooling)
makes 12
tips Meringues can be made 4 days ahead; store at room temperature in an airtight container. Top with cream just before serving.
Persian fairy floss is available from gourmet food stores.

LAVENDER SHORTBREAD

- 250g (8 ounces) unsalted butter, softened
- ⅓ cup (75g) caster (superfine) sugar
- 1 tablespoon water
- 2 cups (300g) plain (all-purpose) flour
- ½ cup (100g) rice flour
- 2 tablespoons dried edible lavender, chopped coarsely
- 2 tablespoons demerara (light brown) sugar

1 Preheat oven to 140°C/280°F. Grease oven trays.

2 Beat butter and caster sugar in small bowl with electric mixer until light and fluffy; transfer to large bowl. Stir in the water, sifted flours and half the lavender, in two batches.

3 Turn dough onto floured surface, knead gently until smooth. Shape dough into two 6cm x 20cm (2¼ inch x 8 inch) rectangular logs; cut into 1cm (½ inch) slices. Place about 2.5cm (1 inch) apart on oven trays; sprinkle with demerara sugar and remaining lavender.

4 Bake shortbread about 20 minutes. Stand 5 minutes; transfer to wire rack to cool.

prep + cook time 40 minutes
makes 32
tip Dried edible lavender is available from specialist cooking stores.

PISTACHIO WHITE CHOCOLATE BRITTLE

2 cups (440g) caster (superfine) sugar
½ cup (125ml) water
2 tablespoons rosewater
1 cup (140g) unsalted, roasted, shelled pistachios, chopped coarsely
1 tablespoon dried rose petals
90g (3 ounces) white eating chocolate, melted

1 Line oven tray with baking paper.
2 Stir sugar and the water in medium saucepan over heat, without boiling, until sugar dissolves. Stir in rosewater; bring to the boil. Boil, uncovered, without stirring, until golden brown. Allow bubbles to subside; add nuts. Pour mixture onto tray; sprinkle with rose petals. Leave to set at room temperature.
3 Turn toffee over; spread chocolate over flat-side of brittle. Leave to set at room temperature. Break brittle into pieces.

prep + cook time 25 minutes (+ standing)
serves 16
tip Dried rose petals are available from specialist cooking stores.

PASSIONFRUIT CREAM BISCUITS

125g (4 ounces) butter, softened
2 teaspoons finely grated lemon rind (peel)
⅓ cup (75g) caster (superfine) sugar
2 tablespoons golden syrup or treacle
1 cup (150g) self-raising flour
⅔ cup (100g) plain (all-purpose) flour
¼ cup (60ml) passionfruit pulp

passionfruit cream

2 tablespoons passionfruit pulp
90g (3 ounces) butter, softened
1 cup (160g) icing (confectioners') sugar

1 Beat butter, rind and sugar in small bowl with electric mixer until light and fluffy. Add golden syrup, beat until combined. Stir in sifted dry ingredients and passionfruit pulp.

2 Turn dough onto floured surface, knead gently until smooth. Cut dough in half; roll each portion between sheets of baking paper to 5mm (¼ inch) thickness. Refrigerate 30 minutes.

3 Preheat oven to 160°C/325°F. Grease oven trays; line with baking paper.

4 Cut 25 x 4cm (1½ inch) fluted rounds from each portion of dough; place about 2.5cm (1 inch) apart on trays.

5 Bake biscuits about 10 minutes. Cool on trays.

6 Meanwhile, make passionfruit cream.

7 Spoon passionfruit cream into piping bag fitted with 5mm (¼ inch) fluted tube. Pipe cream onto half the biscuits; top with remaining biscuits. Serve dusted with a little extra sifted icing sugar, if you like.

passionfruit cream Strain passionfruit pulp through fine sieve into small jug, discard seeds. Beat butter and sugar in small bowl with electric mixer until light and fluffy. Beat in passionfruit juice.

prep + cook time 45 minutes (+ refrigeration & cooling)
makes 25
tip You need about 6 passionfruit for this recipe.

MONTE CARLOS

185g (6 ounces) unsalted butter, softened
1 teaspoon vanilla extract
½ cup (110g) firmly packed light brown sugar
1 egg
1¼ cups (185g) self-raising flour
¾ cup (110g) plain (all-purpose) flour
½ cup (40g) desiccated coconut
½ cup (160g) raspberry jam (conserve)

cream filling

60g (2 ounces) unsalted butter, softened
¾ cup (120g) icing (confectioners') sugar
½ teaspoon vanilla extract
2 teaspoons milk

1 Preheat oven to 160°C/325°F. Grease oven trays.

2 Beat butter, extract and sugar in small bowl with electric mixer until light and fluffy. Add egg, beat until combined. Stir in sifted flours and coconut.

3 Shape level teaspoons of dough into oval shapes; place about 4cm (1½ inch) apart on trays. Rough surface with fork (see page 123).

4 Bake biscuits about 12 minutes. Cool on trays.

5 Meanwhile, make cream filling.

6 Place ½ teaspoon each of jam and cream filling in centre of half the biscuits; top with remaining biscuits, gently press together (see page 123).

cream filling Beat butter and sugar in small bowl with electric mixer until light and fluffy. Beat in extract and milk.

prep + cook time 50 minutes
makes 50

SHORTBREAD CRESCENTS

250g (8 ounces) unsalted butter, softened
1 cup (220g) caster (superfine) sugar
1 egg
¼ cup (60ml) brandy
¾ cup (60g) flaked almonds, roasted, chopped finely
2½ cups (375g) plain (all-purpose) flour
1½ cups (225g) self-raising flour
¼ cup (60ml) orange blossom water
⅓ cup (80ml) water
2 cups (320g) icing (confectioners') sugar

1 Preheat oven to 160°C/325°F. Grease oven trays.
2 Beat butter and sugar in small bowl with electric mixer until light and fluffy. Add egg and brandy, beat until combined; transfer mixture to large bowl. Stir in nuts and sifted flours, in two batches.
3 Turn dough onto floured surface, knead gently until smooth. Shape level tablespoons of dough into crescent shapes; place about 2.5cm (1 inch) apart on trays.
4 Bake shortbread about 15 minutes. Working quickly, place shortbread onto wire racks; brush hot shortbread with combined orange blossom water and the water. Toss shortbread in icing sugar; cool on wire racks.

prep + cook time 50 minutes
makes 45

LINZER BISCUITS

- ⅔ cup (100g) plain (all-purpose) flour
- ⅔ cup (150g) caster (superfine) sugar
- 1½ cups (180g) finely chopped walnuts
- 1 hard-boiled egg yolk
- 90g (3 ounces) butter, chopped coarsely
- 1 egg yolk
- ⅔ cup (220g) fig and ginger jam (conserve)
- 1 tablesp›on icing (confectioners') sugar

1 Combine sifted flour, caster sugar, nuts and hard-boiled egg yolk in medium bowl; rub in butter. Stir in egg yolk until ingredients come together.

2 Turn dough onto floured surface, knead gently until smooth. Cut dough in half; roll each portion between sheets of baking paper to 3mm (⅛ inch) thickness. Refrigerate 30 minutes.

3 Preheat oven to 140°C/280°F. Grease oven trays; line with baking paper.

4 Cut 24 x 5cm (2 inch) fluted rounds from each portion of dough; place about 2.5cm (1 inch) apart on trays. Cut 2.5cm (1 inch) fluted rounds from centre of half the rounds.

5 Bake biscuits about 15 minutes. Cool on trays.

6 Sandwich biscuits with jam. Serve dusted with sifted icing sugar.

prep + cook time 50 minutes (+ refrigeration & cooling)
makes 24
tips The 2cm fluted centre rounds can be baked for about 10 minutes; sandwich with extra jam. You can substitute the fig and ginger jam for any jam of your choice. These biscuits are best served on the day they are made. Store unfilled biscuits in an airtight container for up to 1 week.

All true tea lovers not only like their tea strong,
but like it a little stronger with each year that passes.

– George Orwell A Nice Cup of Tea

LITTLE CAKES

WHITE CHOCOLATE RASPBERRY LAMINGTONS

6 eggs
⅔ cup (150g) caster (superfine) sugar
½ cup (75g) plain (all-purpose) flour
½ cup (75g) self-raising flour
¼ cup (35g) cornflour (cornstarch)
60g (2 ounces) fresh raspberries
4 cups (640g) icing (confectioners') sugar
½ cup (125ml) milk
2 cups (160g) desiccated coconut

white chocolate mousse

125g (4 ounces) white eating chocolate, chopped finely
2 tablespoons thickened (heavy) cream
10g (½ ounce) unsalted butter, chopped
1 egg
1 tablespoon caster (superfine) sugar
¼ cup (60ml) thickened (heavy) cream, whipped, extra

1 Make white chocolate mousse.

2 Preheat oven to 160°C/325°F. Grease deep 22cm (9-inch) square cake pan well with butter; line base and sides with baking paper, extending paper 5cm (2 inch) above sides.

3 Beat eggs and caster sugar in medium bowl with electric mixer for 10 minutes or until thick and creamy.

4 Meanwhile, sift flours twice, then sift over egg mixture; fold ingredients together. Spread mixture into pan.

5 Bake sponge about 35 minutes. Turn sponge immediately onto baking-paper-covered wire rack, then turn top-side up to cool.

6 Cut cake into 25 squares.

7 Blend or process raspberries until smooth; strain through fine sieve into medium heatproof bowl, discard solids. Sift icing sugar into bowl with raspberry puree; stir in milk. Stir over medium saucepan of simmering water until icing is of a coating consistency.

8 Dip a square of cake into icing, drain off excess; toss cake in coconut. Place lamington on wire rack to set. Repeat with remaining cake, icing and coconut.

9 Split each lamington in half; sandwich with mousse.

white chocolate mousse Stir chocolate and cream in small heatproof bowl over small saucepan of simmering water until smooth. Remove from heat; stir in butter. Beat egg and sugar in small bowl with electric mixer until pale and thick; fold egg mixture then extra cream into chocolate mixture. Cover; refrigerate overnight.

prep + cook time 1 hour 20 minutes (+ refrigeration & cooling)
makes 25

MACADAMIA & BANANA LOAVES

2 cups (300g) plain (all-purpose) flour
¾ teaspoon bicarbonate of (baking) soda
¾ cup (165g) firmly packed light brown sugar
½ cup (70g) coarsely chopped macadamias, roasted
¼ cup (10g) flaked coconut, roasted
90g (3 ounces) butter, melted
1½ cups (350g) mashed overripe banana
¼ cup (70g) vanilla yogurt
2 eggs, beaten lightly
1 teaspoon vanilla extract

golden ginger butter

155g (5 ounces) unsalted butter, softened
2 tablespoons golden syrup or treacle
2 teaspoons ground ginger

1 Preheat oven to 160°C/325°F. Grease 12 holes of two 8-hole (¾-cup/180ml) petite loaf pans.

2 Sift flour, soda and sugar into large bowl; mix in nuts and coconut.

3 Combine butter, banana, yogurt, eggs and extract in large jug. Fold banana mixture into flour mixture until combined; do not over mix. Divide mixture into pan holes.

4 Bake loaves about 20 minutes. Stand loaves 5 minutes before turning top-side up onto wire rack to cool.

5 Meanwhile, make golden ginger butter.

6 Cut loaves into thick slices, toast lightly on both sides under hot grill. Serve warm with golden ginger butter.

golden ginger butter Beat butter, syrup and ginger in small bowl with electric mixer until light and fluffy.

prep + cook time 40 minutes (+ cooling)
makes 12
tips You need about 3 large overripe bananas (690g) for the amount of mashed banana in this recipe.
You could cut each loaf into six slices and serve toasted on both sides.

COCONUT ICE CAKES

60g (2 ounces) butter, softened
½ teaspoon coconut essence
½ cup (110g) caster (superfine) sugar
1 egg
¼ cup (20g) desiccated coconut
¾ cup (110g) self-raising flour
½ cup (120g) sour cream
2 tablespoons milk

coconut ice frosting

1 cup (160g) icing (confectioners') sugar
⅔ cup (50g) desiccated coconut
1 egg white, beaten lightly
pink food colouring

1 Preheat oven to 160°C/325°F. Line 18 holes of two 12-hole (2-tablespoons/40ml) deep flat-based patty pans with paper cases.

2 Beat butter, essence, sugar and egg in small bowl with electric mixer until light and fluffy. Stir in the coconut, sifted flour, sour cream and milk, in two batches. Divide mixture into paper cases.

3 Bake cakes about 20 minutes. Stand cakes 5 minutes before turning top-side up onto wire rack to cool.

4 Meanwhile, make coconut ice frosting.

5 Drop alternate rounded teaspoons of white and pink frosting onto cakes; marble over the top of each cake.

coconut ice frosting Sift icing sugar into medium bowl; stir in coconut and egg white. Place half the mixture in small bowl; tint with pink food colouring.

prep + cook time 1 hour (+ cooling)
makes 18
tip Use a hot wet palette knife to spread the frosting over cakes.

MINI SPONGE ROLLS

4 eggs
1¼ cups (150g) ground almonds
1 cup (160g) icing (confectioners') sugar
⅓ cup (50g) plain (all-purpose) flour
30g (1 ounce) unsalted butter, melted
4 egg whites
1 tablespoon caster (superfine) sugar
2 tablespoons desiccated coconut
1 tablespoon white (granulated) sugar
⅔ cup (220g) redcurrant jelly, warmed, strained

mock cream

½ cup (110g) caster (superfine) sugar
¼ cup (60ml) water
1 tablespoon milk
¼ teaspoon gelatine
125g (4 ounces) unsalted butter, softened
1 teaspoon vanilla extract

1 Preheat oven to 200°C/400°F. Mark three 20cm x 25cm (8 inch x 10 inch) rectangles on three sheets baking paper. Grease three oven trays; line with baking paper, marked-side down.

2 Beat eggs, ground almonds and sifted icing sugar in small bowl with electric mixer until creamy; beat in flour. Transfer mixture to large bowl; stir in butter.

3 Beat egg whites in clean small bowl with electric mixer until soft peaks form; add caster sugar, beat until dissolved. Fold into almond mixture, in two batches.

4 Divide mixture between trays, spread inside rectangles (see page 123). Bake, one at a time, about 7 minutes.

5 Meanwhile, cut three pieces of baking paper the same size as the base of 26cm x 32cm (10 inch x 13 inch) swiss roll pan; place paper on bench. Sprinkle one piece of paper with half the coconut, one with half the white sugar and the other with combined remaining coconut and white sugar. Turn each sponge onto baking paper; peel away lining paper. Cut crisp edges from all sides of sponges. Roll sponges from long side, using paper as guide; unroll, then cool (see page 123).

6 Meanwhile, make mock cream.

7 Spread each sponge with cold jelly and mock cream, then re-roll sponges. Cover; refrigerate 30 minutes. Cut each roll into eight slices.

mock cream Stir sugar, 2 tablespoons of the water and milk in small saucepan over low heat, without boiling, until sugar dissolves. Sprinkle gelatine over the remaining water in small jug; stir into milk mixture until gelatine dissolves. Cool. Beat butter and extract in small bowl with electric mixer until as white as possible. Gradually beat in milk mixture until light and fluffy.

prep + cook time 55 minutes (+ refrigeration & cooling)
makes 24

CARROT CAKES

⅓ cup (80ml) vegetable oil
½ cup (110g) firmly packed light brown sugar
1 egg
1 cup firmly packed, coarsely grated carrot
⅓ cup (40g) finely chopped walnuts
¾ cup (110g) self-raising flour
½ teaspoon mixed spice
1 tablespoon pepitas, chopped finely
1 tablespoon finely chopped dried apricots
1 tablespoon finely chopped walnuts, extra

lemon cream cheese frosting

90g (3 ounces) cream cheese, softened
30g (1 ounce) unsalted butter, softened
1 teaspoon finely grated lemon rind (peel)
1½ cups (240g) icing (confectioners') sugar

1 Preheat oven to 160°C/325°F. Line 18 holes of two 12-hole (2-tablespoons/40ml) deep flat-based patty pans with paper cases.
2 Beat oil, sugar and egg in small bowl with electric mixer until thick and creamy. Stir in carrot and walnuts, then sifted flour and spice. Divide mixture into paper cases.
3 Bake cakes about 20 minutes. Stand cakes 5 minutes before turning top-side up onto wire rack to cool.
4 Meanwhile, make lemon cream cheese frosting.
5 Spoon lemon cream cheese frosting into piping bag fitted with 2cm (¾ inch) fluted tube; pipe frosting onto cakes. Sprinkle cakes with combined pepitas, apricots and extra walnuts.

lemon cream cheese frosting
Beat cream cheese, butter and rind in small bowl with electric mixer until light and fluffy; gradually beat in sifted icing sugar.

prep + cook time 45 minutes (+ cooling)
makes 18

FIG & CRANBERRY FRUIT CAKES

60g (2 ounces) butter, softened
¼ cup (55g) firmly packed light brown sugar
1 egg
1 tablespoon orange marmalade
½ cup (80g) sultanas (golden raisins), chopped finely
½ cup (65g) dried cranberries, chopped finely
¼ cup (50g) finely chopped dried figs
¼ cup (40g) dried currants
⅓ cup (50g) plain (all-purpose) flour
2 tablespoons self-raising flour
½ teaspoon mixed spice
¼ cup (60ml) sweet sherry
250g (8 ounces) ready made white icing
2 tablespoons orange marmalade, warmed, strained, extra
24 edible sugar flowers

1 Preheat oven to 130°C/260°F. Line two 12-hole (1-tablespoon/20ml) mini muffin pans with paper cases.

2 Beat butter, sugar and egg in small bowl with electric mixer until combined. Stir in marmalade and fruit, then sifted flours and spice with half the sherry. Divide mixture into paper cases.

3 Bake cakes about 35 minutes. Remove cakes from oven; brush tops with the remaining sherry. Cover pans tightly with foil; cool cakes in pans.

4 On surface dusted with sifted icing sugar, knead white icing until smooth; roll out until 5mm (¼ inch) thick. Cut out 24 x 4cm (1½ inch) fluted round shapes from icing. Brush cold cakes with extra marmalade; top with icing rounds. Brush the bases of the sugar flowers with a little water, push gently into icing.

prep + cook time 1 hour 10 minutes (+ cooling)
makes 24

FIG & WALNUT FRIANDS

1¼ cups (125g) roasted walnuts
6 egg whites
185g (6 ounces) unsalted butter, melted
1½ cups (240g) icing (confectioners') sugar
½ cup (75g) plain (all-purpose) flour
2 teaspoons finely grated orange rind (peel)
1 tablespoon orange juice
4 dried figs (85g), sliced thinly

1 Preheat oven to 180°C/350°F. Grease 12-hole (½-cup/125ml) oval friand pan.
2 Process nuts until ground finely.
3 Place egg whites in medium bowl; whisk lightly with fork until combined. Add butter, sifted icing sugar and flour, rind, juice and nuts; stir until combined. Divide mixture into pans, top with slices of fig.
4 Bake friands about 20 minutes. Stand friands 5 minutes before turning top-side up onto wire rack to cool. Serve dusted with a little sifted icing sugar.

prep + cook time 35 minutes
makes 12

ORANGE BLOSSOM FRIANDS

6 egg whites
185g (6 ounces) unsalted butter, melted
2 tablespoons honey
1 tablespoon orange blossom water
1 cup (120g) ground almonds
1½ cups (240g) icing (confectioners') sugar
½ cup (75g) plain (all-purpose) flour
½ cup (40g) flaked almonds

honey syrup

2 tablespoons honey
1 tablespoon water
2 teaspoons orange blossom water

1 Preheat oven to 180°C/350°F. Grease individual fluted tart moulds (1½-tablespoons/30ml) with butter. Place on oven tray.
2 Place egg whites in medium bowl; whisk lightly with fork until combined. Add butter, honey, orange blossom water, ground almonds, sifted icing sugar and flour; stir until combined. Half fill the tart moulds with mixture; sprinkle with almonds.
3 Bake about 12 minutes. Stand friands 5 minutes before turning top-side up onto wire rack to cool. Repeat with remaining mixture and almonds.
4 Meanwhile, make honey syrup.
5 Serve friands drizzled with honey syrup.

honey syrup Combine honey and the water in small saucepan; bring to the boil. Remove from heat; stir in orange blossom water. Cool.

prep + cook time 35 minutes (+ cooling)
makes 28
tip We used tart moulds bought from a supermarket, which came in sets of four. The friand mixture will be fine left to stand at room temperature if you're making the friands in small batches. Alternatively, make 12 friands using 12-hole (½-cup/125ml) oval friand pan. Divide mixture into pan holes, bake about 20 minutes.

TOFFEE CRUNCH CHEESECAKES

250g (8 ounces) ginger nut biscuits (hard ginger cookies)
90g (3 ounces) unsalted butter, melted
250g (8 ounces) cream cheese, softened
1 teaspoon vanilla extract
¼ cup (55g) firmly packed light brown sugar
¾ cup (180ml) thickened (heavy) cream

buttered pecans

1½ cups (330g) caster (superfine) sugar
½ cup (125ml) water
2 teaspoons glucose syrup
15g (½ ounce) butter
1 tablespoon dark rum
1 cup (120g) pecan halves

1 Grease two 12-hole (1½-tablespoons/30ml) shallow round-based patty pans.

2 Process biscuits until fine. Add butter, process until combined. Divide mixture into pan holes, press firmly and evenly to cover bases of pans. Refrigerate 1 hour.

3 Meanwhile, make buttered pecans.

4 Beat cream cheese, extract and sugar in small bowl with electric mixer until smooth; gradually beat in cream.

5 Divide cream cheese mixture over bases; top with buttered pecans.

buttered pecans Combine sugar, the water and glucose syrup in medium saucepan; stir over heat, without boiling, until sugar dissolves. Bring to the boil; boil, uncovered, without stirring, until mixture reaches 112°C/230°F on a candy thermometer or when small quantity of syrup, dropped into cold water, moulds into a soft ball with fingertips. Add butter and rum; boil, uncovered, for further 12 minutes or until mixture is light golden brown. Remove from heat, drop nuts into pan, do not stir; return to heat for 1 minute. Working quickly and using tongs or a fork, carefully lift nuts out of toffee, one at a time and place on greased oven tray. Set at room temperature; chop coarsely.

prep + cook time 45 minutes (+ refrigeration)
makes 24

JELLY CAKES WITH BERRY CREAM

- 125g (4 ounces) unsalted butter, softened
- ½ cup (110g) caster (superfine) sugar
- 2 teaspoons vanilla extract
- 2 eggs
- 1½ cups (225g) self-raising flour
- ⅓ cup (80ml) milk
- 2 cups (160g) desiccated coconut
- 1¼ cups (300ml) thickened (heavy) cream, whipped
- 1 tablespoon icing (confectioners') sugar
- 1 cup (150g) frozen mixed berries, chopped coarsely
- 25 fresh raspberries

mixed berry jelly

- 1 cup (150g) frozen mixed berries, thawed
- 1½ cups (375ml) apple blackcurrant juice
- ⅓ cup (75g) caster (superfine) sugar
- ¼ cup (60ml) water
- 3 teaspoons gelatine

1 Preheat oven to 160°C/325°F. Grease 22cm (9-inch) square cake pan well with butter; line base with baking paper.

2 Beat butter, caster sugar and half the extract in small bowl with electric mixer until light and fluffy. Beat in eggs, one at a time. Stir in sifted flour and milk, in two batches. Spread mixture into pan.

3 Bake cake about 25 minutes. Stand cake 5 minutes before turning top-side up onto wire rack to cool.

4 Meanwhile, make mixed berry jelly.

5 Trim edges from all sides of cake; cut cake into 25 squares. Dip each square into jelly then roll in coconut. Place on tray, cover; refrigerate 30 minutes.

6 Beat cream, icing sugar and remaining extract in small bowl with electric mixer until soft peaks form; fold in berries. Split each jelly cake in half; sandwich with berry cream. Top each jelly cake with a fresh raspberry.

mixed berry jelly Blend or process berries until smooth. Stir juice, sugar and berry puree in medium saucepan over medium heat until sugar dissolves. Strain mixture through fine sieve; discard solids. Place the water in small heatproof jug; sprinkle over gelatine. Stand jug in small saucepan of simmering water, stirring, until gelatine dissolves. Stir gelatine mixture into berry mixture. Pour into shallow dish; refrigerate, stirring occasionally, until set to the consistency of unbeaten egg white.

prep + cook time 1 hour 10 minutes (+ refrigeration)
makes 25

APPLE CINNAMON TEA LOAVES

90g (3 ounces) butter, softened
1 teaspoon vanilla extract
½ cup (110g) caster (superfine) sugar
1 egg
1⅓ cups (200g) self-raising flour
½ cup (125ml) milk
1 medium red apple (150g), quartered, cored, sliced thinly
15g (½ ounce) butter, melted
1 tablespoon white (granulated) sugar
½ teaspoon ground cinnamon

spiced honey cream

⅔ cup (160ml) double cream
2 teaspoons honey
¼ teaspoon ground ginger
pinch ground cinnamon

1 Preheat oven to 160°C/325°F. Grease 8-hole (¾-cup/180ml) petite loaf pan.

2 Beat softened butter, extract and caster sugar in small bowl with electric mixer until light and fluffy. Add egg, beat until combined. Stir in sifted flour and milk, in two batches.

3 Divide mixture into pan holes; top with apple, brush with melted butter, sprinkle with half the combined white sugar and cinnamon.

4 Bake loaves about 20 minutes. Sprinkle hot loaves with remaining sugar and cinnamon mixture. Stand loaves 5 minutes before turning top-side up onto wire rack to cool.

5 Meanwhile, make spiced honey cream.

6 Serve warm cakes with spiced honey cream.

spiced honey cream Combine ingredients in small bowl.

prep + cook time 35 minutes
makes 8

BLACK FOREST GATEAUX

185g (6 ounces) unsalted butter, softened
1½ cups (330g) caster (superfine) sugar
6 eggs, separated
¾ cup (110g) self-raising flour
⅔ cup (70g) cocoa powder
2 tablespoons milk
½ cup (125ml) blackcurrant liqueur or cherry brandy
1 cup (320g) black cherry jam (conserve)
1¼ cups (300ml) thickened (heavy) cream, whipped
1 cup (200g) seeded drained sour cherries, halved

chocolate ganache

½ cup (125ml) (single) cream
220g (7 ounces) dark eating (semi-sweet) chocolate, chopped coarsely

1 Preheat oven to 160°C/325°F. Grease 20cm x 30cm (8 inch x 12 inch) lamington pan; line with baking paper, extending paper 5cm (2 inch) over long sides.

2 Beat butter, sugar and egg yolks in small bowl with electric mixer until light and fluffy. Stir in sifted flour and cocoa and milk, in two batches.

3 Beat egg whites in clean small bowl with electric mixer until soft peaks form. Fold egg whites into cake mixture, in two batches. Spread mixture into pan.

4 Bake cake about 35 minutes. Stand cake 5 minutes before turning top-side up onto wire rack to cool.

5 Meanwhile, make chocolate ganache.

6 Trim edges from all sides of cake; cut cake into 40 squares. Split each square in half; brush each half with liqueur. Sandwich cakes with jam and cream; top with chocolate ganache and cherries.

chocolate ganache Bring cream to the boil in small saucepan. Remove from heat; pour over chocolate in small bowl, stir until smooth. Stand at room temperature until thickened slightly.

prep + cook time 1 hour 15 minutes (+ cooling)
makes 40

Tea tempers the spirit and harmonises the mind;
dispels lassitude and relieves fatigue,
awakens thought and prevents drowsiness.

– Lu Yu The Sage of Tea

BIG CAKES

ORANGE ALMOND VICTORIA SPONGE

- 185g (6 ounces) unsalted butter, softened
- 1 teaspoon vanilla extract
- ¾ cup (165g) caster (superfine) sugar
- 3 eggs
- ¼ cup (60ml) milk
- 1½ cups (225g) self-raising flour
- 1 cup (320g) orange marmalade, warmed
- 1¼ cups (300ml) thickened (heavy) cream
- 2 tablespoons icing (confectioners') sugar
- ½ cup (40g) flaked almonds, roasted

1 Preheat oven to 160°C/325°F. Grease deep 20cm (8-inch) ring pan well with butter.

2 Beat butter, extract, and caster sugar in small bowl with electric mixer until light and fluffy. Beat in eggs, one at a time. Stir in milk and sifted flour, in two batches.

3 Spread mixture into pan; bake about 30 minutes. Turn sponge immediately onto baking-paper-covered wire rack, turn top-side up to cool.

4 Meanwhile, strain marmalade through fine sieve; reserve syrup and rind separately.

5 Beat cream and half the icing sugar in small bowl with electric mixer until soft peaks form.

6 Split sponge into three layers. Place one layer onto serving plate, cut-side up; spread with half of the marmalade syrup. Top with another layer of sponge and remaining syrup; top with remaining layer of sponge. Cut sponge into twelve pieces, keeping cake in ring shape.

7 Spread two-thirds of the cream around side of sponge; press almonds into cream. Spoon remaining cream into piping bag fitted with 1cm (½ inch) fluted tube. Pipe rosettes on top of cake; top with some of the reserved rind. Serve sponge dusted with remaining icing sugar.

prep + cook time 55 minutes (+ cooling)
serves 12

PINK VELVET CAKE

125g (4 ounces) butter, softened
1 teaspoon vanilla extract
1½ cups (330g) caster (superfine) sugar
2 eggs
1½ cups (225g) plain (all-purpose) flour
2 tablespoons cornflour (cornstarch)
2 tablespoons cocoa powder
1 cup (250ml) buttermilk
1 tablespoon rose pink food colouring
1 teaspoon white vinegar
1 teaspoon bicarbonate of (baking) soda
1 cup (50g) flaked coconut

mascarpone frosting

250g (8 ounces) cream cheese, softened
250g (8 ounces) mascarpone cheese
1 cup (160g) icing (confectioners') sugar
1 teaspoon vanilla extract
1¼ cups (300ml) thickened (heavy) cream

1 Preheat oven to 160°C/325°F. Grease two deep 23cm (9-inch) round cake pans; line bases and sides with baking paper.

2 Beat butter, extract, sugar and eggs in small bowl with electric mixer until light and fluffy. Transfer mixture to large bowl; stir in sifted flours and cocoa and combined buttermilk and food colouring, in two batches.

3 Combine vinegar and soda in a cup; allow to fizz then fold into cake mixture. Divide mixture between pans.

4 Bake cakes about 25 minutes. Stand cakes 10 minutes before turning top-side up onto wire rack to cool. Enclose cakes in plastic wrap; freeze 40 minutes.

5 Meanwhile, make mascarpone frosting.

6 Split cold cakes in half. Place one layer on serving plate, cut-side up; spread with ⅔ cup frosting. Repeat layering, finishing with remaining frosting spread over top and side of cake; press coconut onto side of cake.

mascarpone frosting Beat cream cheese, mascarpone, sugar and extract in small bowl with electric mixer until smooth. Beat in cream.

prep + cook time 1 hour (+ cooling & freezing)
serves 12
tip To make your own buttermilk equivalent, combine 1 tablespoon fresh lemon juice with enough reduced-fat milk to make 1 cup. Stand a few minutes until thickened; stir.

RASPBERRY CREAM SPONGE

4 eggs
¾ cup (165g) caster (superfine) sugar
⅔ cup (100g) wheaten cornflour (cornstarch)
¼ cup (30g) custard powder (instant pudding mix)
1 teaspoon cream of tartar
½ teaspoon bicarbonate of (baking) soda
¾ cup (240g) raspberry jam (conserve)
1½ cups (375ml) thickened (heavy) cream, whipped

raspberry glacé icing

45g (1½ ounces) fresh raspberries
2 cups (320g) icing (confectioners') sugar
15g (½ ounce) butter, softened
2 teaspoons hot water, approximately

1 Preheat oven to 160°C/325°F. Grease deep 22cm (9-inch) square cake pan with butter.

2 Beat eggs and sugar in small bowl with electric mixer about 10 minutes or until thick and creamy and sugar has dissolved; transfer to large bowl.

3 Sift dry ingredients twice, then sift over egg mixture; fold dry ingredients into egg mixture. Spread mixture into pan.

4 Bake sponge about 25 minutes. Turn sponge immediately onto baking-paper-covered wire rack, then turn top-side up to cool.

5 Meanwhile, make raspberry glacé icing.

6 Split sponge in half. Sandwich with jam and cream. Spread sponge with icing, sprinkle with fresh rose petals.

raspberry glacé icing Push raspberries through fine sieve into small heatproof bowl; discard solids. Sift icing sugar into same bowl; stir in butter and enough of the water to make a thick paste. Place bowl over small saucepan of simmering water; stir until icing is spreadable.

prep + cook time 50 minutes (+ cooling)
serves 16
tip Use a serrated or electric knife to split and cut the sponge.

MIXED BERRY HAZELNUT CAKE

250g (8 ounces) unsalted butter, softened
1½ cups (330g) caster (superfine) sugar
6 eggs
1 cup (150g) plain (all-purpose) flour
½ cup (75g) self-raising flour
1 cup (110g) ground hazelnuts
⅔ cup (160g) sour cream
300g (10 ounces) fresh mixed berries

white chocolate ganache

¾ cup (180ml) thickened (heavy) cream
1 tablespoon blackcurrant-flavoured liqueur
375g (12 ounces) white eating chocolate, chopped coarsely

sugared berries

125g (4 ounces) fresh raspberries
125g (4 ounces) fresh blueberries
1 egg white, beaten lightly
¼ cup (55g) caster (superfine) sugar

1 Make white chocolate ganache.

2 Preheat oven to 160°C/325°F. Grease deep 23cm x 31cm (9 inch x 12 inch) oval cake pan; line base and side with baking paper.

3 Beat butter and sugar in small bowl with electric mixer until light and fluffy. Beat in eggs, one at a time. Transfer mixture to large bowl; stir in sifted flours, ground hazelnuts, sour cream and berries. Spread mixture into pan.

4 Bake cake about 1½ hours. Stand cake 10 minutes before turning top-side up onto wire rack to cool.

5 Meanwhile, make sugared berries.

6 Spread cake with ganache; top with sugared berries.

white chocolate ganache Bring cream and liqueur to the boil in medium saucepan. Remove from heat; pour over chocolate in small bowl, stir until smooth. Cover; refrigerate overnight. Beat ganache in small bowl with electric mixer until mixture changes to paler colour.

sugared berries Using small artists paint brush, brush berries very lightly with egg white; toss in sugar. Place in a single layer on tray; allow to dry at room temperature.

prep + cook time 2 hours (+ refrigeration)
serves 24
tip You can use frozen berries in the cake mixture, use them while they're still frozen.

TIRAMISU TORTE

3 eggs
½ cup (110g) caster (superfine) sugar
¼ cup (35g) plain (all-purpose) flour
¼ cup (35g) self-raising flour
¼ cup (35g) pure cornflour (cornstarch)
2 tablespoons instant coffee granules
¾ cup (180ml) boiling water
⅓ cup (80ml) marsala
2 tablespoons coffee-flavoured liqueur
500g (1 pound) mascarpone cheese
⅓ cup (55g) icing (confectioners') sugar
1¼ cups (300ml) thickened (heavy) cream

1 Preheat oven to 160°C/325°F. Grease deep 22cm (9-inch) square cake pan with butter.
2 Beat eggs in small bowl with electric mixer about 10 minutes or until thick and creamy; gradually add caster sugar, one tablespoon at a time, beating until sugar dissolves between additions. Transfer to large bowl.
3 Sift flours twice. Sift flours over egg mixture; fold ingredients together. Spread mixture into pan.
4 Bake sponge about 25 minutes. Turn sponge immediately onto baking-paper-covered wire rack, turn top-side up to cool.
5 Meanwhile, dissolve coffee in the water in small heatproof jug. Stir in marsala and liqueur; cool.
6 Beat mascarpone and icing sugar in small bowl with electric mixer until smooth. Beat in cream and ⅓ cup of the coffee mixture.
7 Split sponge in half vertically then each sponge in half horizontally. Place one of the cake rectangles on serving plate, cut-side up; brush with a quarter of the remaining coffee mixture then spread with ⅔ cup of mascarpone mixture. Repeat layering process finishing with the cake, cut-side down, and remaining mascarpone mixture spread on top and sides of cake. Refrigerate cake 2 hours.
8 Decorate cake with coarsely chopped vienna almonds, if you like.

prep + cook time 1 hour 10 minutes (+ cooling & refrigeration)
serves 12
tip Alternate the sponge pieces when layering so that the cut side of the sponge is on different sides on each layer; this will ensure the torte is even and does not lean to one side.

Radish sandwiches with green onion butter (page 12)
Spread butter mixture over one side of eight bread slices; top four slices with half the radish. Spread butter mixture over both sides of four more bread slices.

Top radish layer with a double-buttered bread slice, layer more radishes on top; sandwich with a single-buttered bread slice.

Vanilla bean scones (page 19)
Knead scone dough until smooth on floured surface. Gently press dough out to an even thickness to make a 20cm (8-inch) square.

Dip the blade of a sharp knife into flour, cut the square of dough into 16 even squares.

Date scones with whipped caramel butter (page 20)
Knead scone dough until smooth on floured surface. Gently press dough out to an even thickness to make a 20cm (8-inch) square.

Dip the blade of a sharp knife into flour, cut the square of dough into nine even squares. Cut each square in half diagonally. Position triangles in pan.

Rhubarb frangipane tarts (page 48)
Using sharp knife, cut thawed pastry sheet into quarters, then cut each quarter into three rectangles.

Spread almond mixture over rectangles, leaving a border; position rhubarb on top. Fold edges of pastry up to border the rhubarb.

Orange & almond palmiers (page 35)
Roll one sheet of the thawed pastry over the sugared surface without stretching or changing the shape of the pastry.

Spread half the nut mixture evenly over pastry. Fold one side of pastry over to the centre of the sheet. Fold opposite side of pastry over to meet the first fold in the middle.

Flatten folded pastry slightly, brush with egg. Fold each side over again to meet in the middle, flatten slightly, brush with egg.

Gently fold pastry in half, place folded-side down on surface before cutting into palmiers.

Monte carlos (page 78)
Shape biscuit dough into ovals, place about 4cm (1½ inch) apart on greased oven trays. Use a fork to rough the surface of the biscuits.

Join cooled biscuits with ½ teaspoon each of the jam and the cream filling; gently press together.

Mini sponge rolls (page 92)
Draw three rectangles on three pieces baking paper; place paper, marked-side down, on oven trays. Spread sponge mixture within marked rectangles.

Trim crisp edges from all sides of each hot sponge. Using prepared baking paper as a guide, roll each sponge, then unroll and cool.

GLOSSARY

almonds
flaked paper thin almond slices.
ground also called almond meal.
vienna toffee-coated almonds.

baking powder a raising agent consisting mainly of two parts cream of tartar to one part bicarbonate of soda.

bicarbonate of soda also known as baking soda.

butter we use salted butter unless stated otherwise; 125g is equal to 1 stick (4 ounces).

buttermilk originally the term given to the slightly sour liquid left after butter was churned from cream, today it is made similarly to yogurt. Sold alongside fresh milk products in supermarkets. Despite the implication of its name, buttermilk is low in fat.

capers the grey-green buds of a warm climate (usually Mediterranean) shrub, sold either dried and salted or pickled in a vinegar brine; baby capers are also available both in brine or dried in salt.

cheese
mascarpone an Italian fresh cultured-cream product made in much the same way as yogurt. Whiteish to creamy yellow in colour, with a buttery-rich, luscious texture. Soft, creamy and spreadable, it is used in many Italian desserts and as an accompaniment to a dessert of fresh fruit.
parmesan also called parmigiano; a hard, grainy cow-milk cheese originating in Parma, Italy.

chocolate
dark eating made of cocoa liquor, cocoa butter and sugar.
white eating contains no cocoa solids but derives its sweet flavour from cocoa butter. Very sensitive to heat.

cinnamon available in pieces (sticks or quills) and in ground form; is one of the most common spices.

cloves dried flower buds of a tropical tree; can be used whole or in ground form. Has a strong scent and taste, so should be used minimally.

cocoa powder also known as unsweetened cocoa.

coconut
desiccated concentrated, dried, unsweetened and finely shredded coconut flesh.
shredded unsweetened thin strips of dried coconut flesh.

coconut-flavoured liqueur we used Malibu.

cornflour also known as cornstarch. Available made from corn or wheat (wheaten cornflour, gluten-free, gives a lighter texture in cakes).

cos lettuce also called romaine; the traditional caesar salad lettuce. Long, with leaves ranging from dark green on the outside to almost white near the core; the leaves have a stiff centre rib giving a slight cupping effect to the leaf on either side.

cream we use fresh pouring cream (pure cream). It has no additives and contains a minimum fat content of 35%.
thickened a whipping cream that contains a thickener. Has a minimum fat content of 35%.

cream of tartar the acid ingredient in baking powder; added to confectionery mixtures to help prevent sugar from crystallising. Keeps frostings creamy and improves volume when beating egg whites.

crème fraîche a mature, naturally fermented cream (minimum fat content 35%) with a velvety texture and slightly tangy, nutty flavour. A French variation of sour cream, it can boil without curdling and can be used in sweet and savoury dishes.

custard powder instant mixture used to make pouring custard; similar to North American instant pudding mixes.

dill also called dill weed; used fresh or dried, in seed form or ground. Its anise/celery sweetness flavours the food of the Scandinavian countries, Germany and Greece. Distinctive feathery, frond-like fresh leaves are grassier and more subtle than the dried version of the seeds (which slightly resemble caraway in flavour).

dried cranberries dried sweetened cranberries; commercially labelled as craisins.

eggs if recipes call for raw or barely cooked eggs, exercise caution if there is a salmonella problem in your area, particularly for children and pregnant women.

flour
plain also called all-purpose flour.
rice very fine, almost powdery, gluten-free flour; made from ground white rice. Used in baking, as a thickener, and in some Asian noodles and desserts.
self-raising all-purpose plain or wholemeal flour with baking powder and salt added; make at home in the proportion of 1 cup plain flour to 2 teaspoons baking powder.

food colouring vegetable-based substance available in liquid, paste or gel form.

gelatine a thickening agent. We use powdered gelatine; is also available in sheets known as leaf gelatine.
ginger
glacé fresh ginger root preserved in sugar syrup; crystallised ginger can be substituted if rinsed with warm water and dried before use.
ground also called powdered ginger; used as a flavouring in baking but cannot be substituted for fresh ginger.
glacé fruit fruit such as peaches, pineapple, orange and citron cooked in heavy syrup then dried.
glucose syrup also called liquid glucose; a sugar syrup made from starches such as wheat and corn.
golden syrup a by-product of refined sugarcane; pure maple syrup or honey can be substituted.
hazelnuts also called filberts; plump, grape-size, rich, sweet nut with a brown inedible skin that is removed by rubbing heated nuts together vigorously in a tea-towel.
meal is made by grounding hazelnuts to a coarse flour.
lebanese cucumbers short, slender and thin-skinned. Probably the most popular variety because of its tender, edible skin, tiny, yielding seeds, and sweet, fresh and flavoursome taste.
limoncello liqueur Italian lemon-flavoured liqueur; originally made from the juice and peel of lemons grown along the Amalfi coast.
macadamias native to Australia; fairly large, slightly soft, buttery rich nut. Should always be stored in the fridge to prevent their high oil content turning them rancid.
marsala a fortified Italian wine produced in the region surrounding the Sicilian city of Marsala; recognisable by its intense amber colour and complex aroma. Often used in cooking, especially in sauces, risottos and desserts.
mayonnaise we use whole-egg mayonnaise unless specified.
milk, sweetened condensed a canned milk product consisting of milk with more than half the water content removed and sugar added to the milk that remains.
mixed spice a classic spice mixture generally containing caraway, allspice, coriander, cumin, nutmeg and ginger.
mustard, dijon also called french. Pale brown, creamy, distinctively flavoured, fairly mild french mustard.
oil, vegetable any number of oils from plant rather than animal fats.
orange blossom water concentrated flavouring made from orange blossoms.
orange-flavoured liqueur brandy-based liqueur such as Grand Marnier or Cointreau.
pepitas are the pale green kernels of dried pumpkin seeds; they can be bought plain or salted.
pomegranate dark-red, leathery-skinned fresh fruit about the size of an orange, filled with hundreds of seeds wrapped in an edible lucent-crimson pulp having a unique tangy sweet-sour flavour.
ready made white icing prepared fondant; available in supermarkets.
rhubarb a plant with long, green-red stalks; becomes sweet and edible when cooked.
rocket also called arugula, rugula and rucola; peppery green leaf, eaten raw in salads or used in cooking. Baby rocket leaves are smaller and less peppery.
rosewater extract made from crushed rose petals; used for its aromatic quality in many desserts.
sugar
brown an extremely soft, fine granulated sugar retaining molasses for its characteristic colour and flavour.
caster also known as superfine or finely granulated table sugar. The fine crystals dissolve easily so it is perfect for cakes, meringues and desserts.
demerara small-grained golden-coloured crystal sugar.
icing also called confectioners' sugar or powdered sugar; pulverised granulated sugar crushed with a small amount (about 3%) of cornflour.
pure icing also called confectioners' sugar or powdered sugar.
white coarse, granulated table sugar, also known as crystal sugar.
vanilla
bean dried long, thin pod from a tropical golden orchid grown in central and South America and Tahiti; the miniscule black seeds inside the bean are used to impart a sweet vanilla flavour to baking and in desserts.
extract vanilla beans that have been submerged in alcohol. Vanilla essence is not a suitable substitute.
watercress one of the cress family, a large group of peppery greens used raw in salads, dips and sandwiches, or cooked in soups. Highly perishable, so it must be used as soon as possible after purchase.
yogurt we use plain full-cream yogurt unless stated otherwise.

INDEX

CONVERSION CHART

measures

One Australian metric measuring cup holds approximately 250ml; one Australian metric tablespoon holds 20ml; one Australian metric teaspoon holds 5ml.

The difference between one country's measuring cups and another's is within a two- or three-teaspoon variance, and will not affect your cooking results. North America, New Zealand and the United Kingdom use a 15ml tablespoon.

All cup and spoon measurements are level. The most accurate way of measuring dry ingredients is to weigh them. When measuring liquids, use a clear glass or plastic jug with metric markings.

We use large eggs with an average weight of 60g.

dry measures

METRIC	IMPERIAL
15g	½oz
30g	1oz
60g	2oz
90g	3oz
125g	4oz (¼lb)
155g	5oz
185g	6oz
220g	7oz
250g	8oz (½lb)
280g	9oz
315g	10oz
345g	11oz
375g	12oz (¾lb)
410g	13oz
440g	14oz
470g	15oz
500g	16oz (1lb)
750g	24oz (1½lb)
1kg	32oz (2lb)

liquid measures

METRIC	IMPERIAL
30ml	1 fluid oz
60ml	2 fluid oz
100ml	3 fluid oz
125ml	4 fluid oz
150ml	5 fluid oz
190ml	6 fluid oz
250ml	8 fluid oz
300ml	10 fluid oz
500ml	16 fluid oz
600ml	20 fluid oz
1000ml (1 litre)	32 fluid oz

length measures

3mm	⅛in
6mm	¼in
1cm	½in
2cm	¾in
2.5cm	1in
5cm	2in
6cm	2½in
8cm	3in
10cm	4in
13cm	5in
15cm	6in
18cm	7in
20cm	8in
23cm	9in
25cm	10in
28cm	11in
30cm	12in (1ft)

oven temperatures

These are fan-forced temperatures. If you have a conventional oven (ie. not fan-forced), increase temperatures by 10-20°.

	°C (CELSIUS)	°F (FAHRENHEIT)	GAS MARK
Very slow	100	210	½
Slow	130	260	1-2
Moderately slow	140	280	3
Moderate	160	325	4-5
Moderately hot	180	350	6
Hot	200	400	7-8
Very hot	220	425	9